A Therapy Resource published by Upbility

 PART 2

DEVELOPMENT
Of Reading
Comprehension
In children with
Autism
Spectrum
Disorder

Kassotaki Alice – Speech-Language Pathologist MSc, BSc

Upbility Publications LTD | 81-83 Grivas Digenis Avenue, Nicosia, 1090 Cyprus

E-mail: info@upbility.eu

www.upbility.net

SKU: EN-EB1062

Author: Alice Kassotaki – *Speech-Language Pathologist MSc, BSc*

Translation & Proofreading: Rigli Maria

Table of contents

Theoretical Background

Practice Activities

Reading comprehension, definition

Reading comprehension is a complex process consisting of complicated mental and psychological operations, including memory, perception and recall of information and meanings found in long-term memory. Furthermore, it involves distinct skills related to language competence, listening comprehension and general intelligence.

Factors of reading comprehension

Reading comprehension is influenced by mental functioning, knowledge and oral language. The basic factors of reading comprehension are the following:

❖ **Motivation to learn:** Motivation is what pushes, incites, influences and drives learners to increase their knowledge. It activates a series of processes that affect a learner's performance in several ways.

❖ **Attention/Concentration:** When a learner pays attention to what they read and concentrates on it, they can understand it in depth and remember it more easily.

❖ **Processing speed/rate:** When learners process auditory and visual information at a quick rate, they can analyze the meaning of what they have read with more ease.

❖ **Vocabulary:** Knowing the significance of words helps learners to enhance the receptive vocabulary and allows them to understand a text more easily.

❖ **Critical thinking:** During reading, learners should make and reject assumptions about the meaning of a text.

❖ **Precision/Fluency:** When these reading skills are automated, learners can read sentences that are syntactically more complex. The processes of word recognition and reading comprehension are automated.

❖ **Decoding:** Decoding words is essential to understanding a text in its entirety. The two processes are inseparable.

❖ **Memory:** Learners can remember the information of the text they have read, and summarize it more easily, in order to understand its meaning.

Factors of reading comprehension

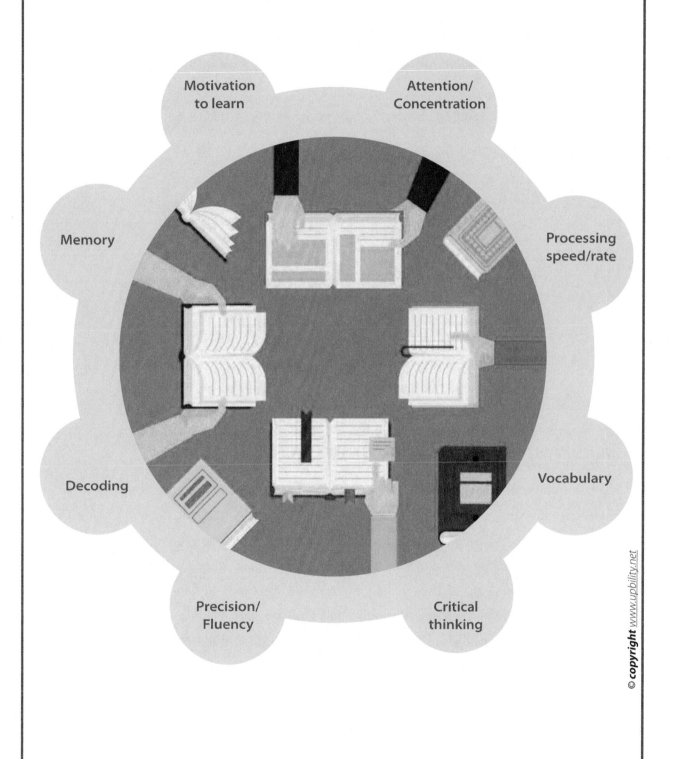

- Motivation to learn
- Attention/Concentration
- Memory
- Processing speed/rate
- Decoding
- Vocabulary
- Precision/Fluency
- Critical thinking

Schema

Types of reading comprehension

There are three types of reading comprehension:

Passive comprehension, which does not aim at the in-depth analysis of the text

Understanding for learning, in which attention is focused on details and on the meaning inferred from the text

Self-regulated understanding, in which readers achieve their personal goals – connection of existing knowledge

Development of reading comprehension

Reading comprehension is, as mentioned above, a complex and multifaceted process. As a result, readers do not develop reading comprehension directly, easily, independently and quickly. The results of this process become evident over time. Reading comprehension strategies must be taught over an extended period of time by parents, teachers and experts who have the relevant knowledge and experience. They must be improved, practised and reinforced continually throughout life. Parents and teachers must keep on helping children to develop reading comprehension strategies, even at a secondary education level. At this level, reading materials become more complex and difficult to understand, which requires children to learn to use new tools for understanding these texts. The development of reading comprehension is a lifelong process that changes based on the depth and breadth of texts a person is reading.

Reading comprehension components

Reading comprehension is the ultimate goal of reading. It entails three elements:

❖ **The reader who should comprehend:** The reader should have a wide range of cognitive, motivational and linguistic abilities and capacities, including attention, memory, critical analytical thinking, inferencing and visualization skills, vocabulary, language and motor skills, interest in the content and reading self-efficacy.

❖ **The text that is to be comprehended:** The characteristics of a text can have a large effect on comprehension. During reading, readers construct different representations of the text that are essential to comprehension.

❖ **The activity in which comprehension is a part:** Reading is done for a purpose; something must be achieved. Activity refers to this dimension of reading. A reading activity involves one or more purposes.

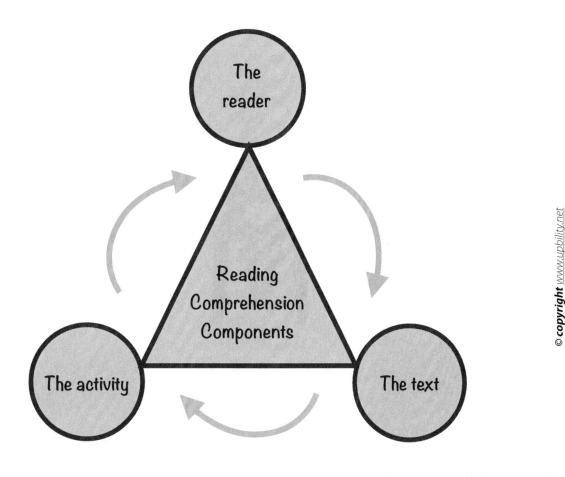

Reading comprehension and autism

According to scientific research, children acquire decoding and reading comprehension skills at the same time, but each skill develops independently of the other. Children with autism spectrum disorder (ASD) usually develop decoding skills, but have difficulty with reading comprehension. They can identify words relatively more easily than understanding what they have read. This may be attributed to the fact that comprehension is a more abstract skill than decoding.

Learners with autism can read and process written language in a fluent way, in contrast to children with dyslexia who often try hard to decode written language. However, these children are not always able to approach semantic meaning in the same way. They can have trouble visualizing action and understanding the social interactions upon which many storylines rely. A detail might absorb all their attention and prevent them from fully processing the rest of the text.

The cycle of reading comprehension difficulties

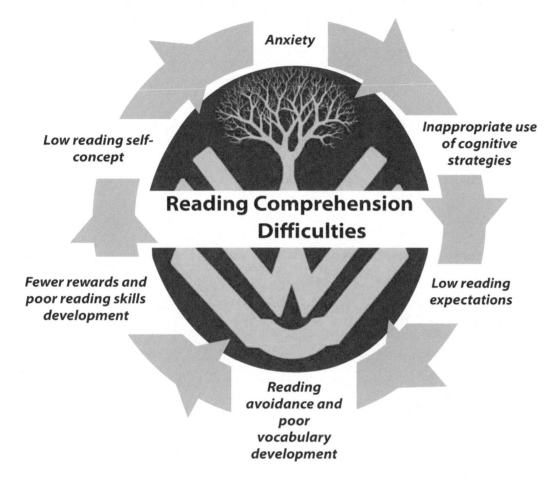

Anxiety

Inappropriate use of cognitive strategies

Low reading self-concept

Reading Comprehension Difficulties

Fewer rewards and poor reading skills development

Low reading expectations

Reading avoidance and poor vocabulary development

The above schema shows the complex nature of reading comprehension difficulties and the way in which it is associated with reading skills development. A child with reading difficulty problems may not be sure of their reading skills and may feel anxious about reading tasks. This anxiety may entail an appropriate use of strategies implemented during reading. Reading failure can contribute to lower reading expectations by the reader. This, in turn, may lead to avoidance of reading, resulting in reduced vocabulary development and a widening gap in performance as compared to other more successful readers. Reading difficulties and poor skills development are generally connected with fewer rewards. When children with poor reading skills compare themselves to other skilled readers in the classroom, they may think bad of themselves or start to have low self-esteem/self-concept. Thus, what may have started as a simple problem may over time develop into a complex cycle of reading failure and influence other personality traits.

Reading comprehension strategies

Strategies are not distinct behaviours. Children use them in many different ways and combine or incorporate them whenever they find it difficult to understand a text. Vocabulary knowledge and the interpretation of what has been read have a key position in all strategies.

(1) **Activating prior knowledge or making connections.** Readers recall knowledge that has already been gained about the world, the words and the texts. They make associations; they apply this prior knowledge to understand the new knowledge offered by a text.

(2) **Making and verifying assumptions or predictions.** Readers make assumptions about the texts before and during reading. Their assumptions will help them to make predictions. If they are good readers, they are going to check them with the new information in the text, in order to verify or revise these predictions. The assumptions can be based on any aspect of the text, such as the text structure, the subject matter, the size and shape of a text, or the context and the task within which the reading is required.

(3) **Identifying main ideas.** Readers determine the most important or central ideas of the text. For this purpose, they draw on their prior knowledge and experience of the ways in which texts are structured (for example, they can use the knowledge that newspaper articles often state the main idea in the first sentence) to infer meaning and determine the relevant importance. Readers may also hypothesize and synthesize different aspects of the text in order to identify the main idea.

(4) **Knowledge of the structure of the text.** The way in which a text is structured plays a major role in comprehension. Readers can use what they already know or what they are learning about the structure of the text in order to navigate and comprehend new texts.

Reading comprehension strategies

(5) **Summarizing.** Readers make rapid summaries (rather like making mental notes) of what they are reading as they work through a text, checking for connections and explanations. In other words, they use their knowledge of topics, vocabulary and text structure to find and connect the important points of the text.

(6) **Drawing conclusions.** Readers make assumptions to fill in gaps, as they read, trying to infer the information that the writer has not made explicit. To do this, readers rely on their background knowledge, testing hypotheses about the writer's intentions.

(7) **Creating mental images or visualizing.** During reading, readers construct mental images, in order to represent the ideas or the information in ways that help them relate them to their own knowledge. They also use mental images to help them discover, for example, patterns in ideas or text structure. This process will enable a deeper understanding of the text.

(8) **Asking questions about the text and seeking answers.** Most readers always use the strategy of posing and answering questions, when they read a text, as this can help them understand its content. Questions may relate to the meanings of words or sentences, to the structure of the text as a whole, to the plot or character development in a story, or to any other aspect of the text and its context. Through asking questions, readers are able to form and test hypotheses, to make inferences, to summarize and coordinate the use of other comprehension strategies.

Content structure

Reading comprehension difficulties are associated with deficits in a wide range of cognitive and mental processes. In the case of most learners with special educational needs, the main causes of these problems are mostly unknown. It is accepted that reading comprehension skills require the reader to be able to process the written symbols of a text, at an appropriate rate and level of precision. However, this is not enough. Reading and comprehension necessitate active involvement. Comprehension is, actually, a complex, interactive process of perceiving, processing, retaining and using the meaning or the semantic content of the word, the sentence or the text that is spoken or written.

The e-book "Developing Reading Comprehension in Children with Autism Spectrum Disorder" is intended for children with severe difficulties in comprehending texts. It proposes six levels of intervention, selected based on scaling difficulty.

These levels comprise various activities:

1. *The first level comprises activities for the development of reading comprehension of words. Children are asked to read some words, understand their meaning, circle them and match them to the appropriate pictures. There are 64 words for reading comprehension.*

2. *The second level comprises activities for the development of reading comprehension of phrases. Children are asked to read some phrases, understand their meaning and match them to the appropriate pictures. There are 64 phrases for reading comprehension.*

3. *The third level comprises activities for the development of reading comprehension of sentences. Children are asked to read some sentences, understand their meaning and match them to the appropriate pictures. There are 33 sentences for reading comprehension.*

4. *The fourth level comprises activities for the development of reading comprehension of texts. Children read a text that has four sentences. Then they listen to or read some questions. They are given two answers and are asked to select and circle the correct one. There are 34 texts for reading comprehension.*

Content structure

5   *The fifth level comprises activities for the reading comprehension of texts. Children read a text that has four sentences. Then they listen to or read questions and write down their answers. There are 22 texts for reading comprehension.*

6   *The sixth level comprises activities for the development of reading comprehension of texts. Children read a text that has six sentences. Then they listen to or read questions and write down their answers. There are 24 reading comprehension activities.*

Level 1

At the first level of reading comprehension, children are asked to read some words independently, understand their meaning and circle the word that matches the picture. The words that children should read and recognise are the following:

Persons:	Animals:	Places:	Feelings:	Actions:	Colours:
a girl	*a cat*	*a school*	*happy*	*play tennis*	*white*
a boy	*a dog*	*a house*	*sad*	*play basketball*	*black*
a man	*a pig*	*a market*	*scared*	*dance*	*red*
a woman	*a frog*	*a park*	*terrified*	*eat*	*yellow*
	an elephant	*a forest*	*angry*	*swim*	*blue*
	a sheep	*sea*	*tired*	*cook*	*brown*
	a monkey	*a kitchen*		*be in pain*	*grey*
	a horse	*haidresser's*		*write*	*orange*
		a court		*read*	*pink*
		a bus		*cut one's hair*	
		a boat		*sit*	
		a river		*run*	
		a lake		*take a photo*	
		a mountain		*listen to music*	
				fish	

Instructions: *Read the words and circle the one that matches the picture of each frame.*

a boy

a girl

a man

a woman

a woman

a man

a boy

a girl

Instructions: *Read the words and draw a line linking up each word with the corresponding pictures.*

•   • **a boy**

•   • **a girl**

•   • **a man**

•   • **a woman**

Instructions: *Read the words and circle the one that matches the picture of each frame.*

a duck

a pig

a frog

a fox

a mouse

a cat

a dog

a bird

•   • a cat

•   • a dog

•   • a pig

•   • a frog

a horse

a fox

a monkey

a cat

a sheep

a fish

a zebra

an elephant

•   • an elephant

•   • a sheep

•   • a monkey

•   • a horse

a house

a school

a house

a forest

a river

the sea

a mountain

a house

Instructions: *Read the words and draw a line linking up each word with the corresponding pictures.*

•   • a house

•   • a school

•   • a forest

•   • a river

an airplane

a bus

a park

a house

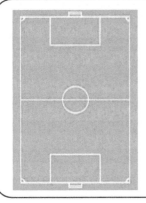

a yard

a field

a living room

a kitchen

 •

• a park

 •

• a bus

 •

• a kitchen

 •

• a field

Instructions: Read the words and circle the one that matches the picture of each frame.

a living room

a lake

a mountain

a river

a house

the sea

a car

a boat

Instructions: *Read the words and draw a line linking up each word with the corresponding pictures.*

•   • a boat

•   • a lake

•   • a mountain

•   • the sea

a forest

a house

a lake

the sky

a market

a school

the hairdresser's

the sea

•

• the hairdresser's

•

• the sky

•

• a market

•

• a house

Instructions: *Read the words and circle the one that matches the picture of each frame.*

 scared

happy

 happy

sad

 happy

scared

 angry

happy

•   • happy

•   • angry

•   • sad

•   • scared

Instructions: *Read the words and draw a line linking up each word with the corresponding pictures.*

• •tired

• •scared

• •happy

• •sad

dance

sleep

eat

drink

give a present

sit

play tennis

eat

• play tennis

• buy a present

• dance

• eat ice cream

write

play

be in pain

drink

sleep

cook

walk

swim

●   ● swim

●   ● cook

●   ● be in pain

●   ● write

cut
someone's
hair

walk

eat

read

play

sleep

sit

laugh

Instructions: *Read the words and draw a line linking up each word with the corresponding pictures.*

• read

• cut someone's hair

• sit

• play basketball

hear

bend

run

sleep

walk

take a photo

fish

swim

Instructions: *Read the words and draw a line linking up each word with the corresponding pictures.*

•   • run

•   • take a photo

•   • listen to music

•   • fish

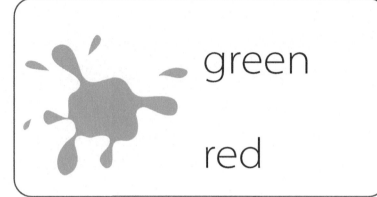

green

red

white

blue

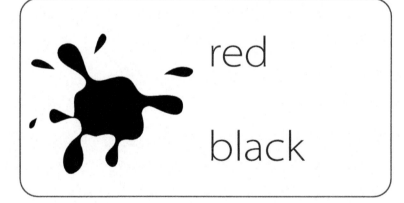

red

black

red

yellow

•   • red

•   • green

•   • white

•   • black

Instructions: *Read the words and circle the one that matches the picture of each frame.*

blue

green

red

pink

brown

yellow

orange

black

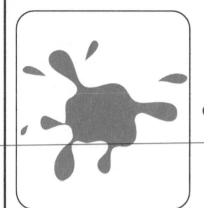

•   • yellow

•   • blue

•   • orange

•   • pink

Instructions: *Read the words and circle the one that matches the picture of each frame.*

blue

grey

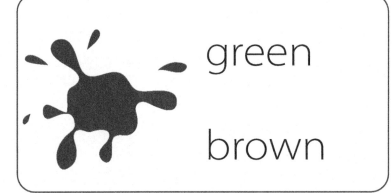

green

brown

white

black

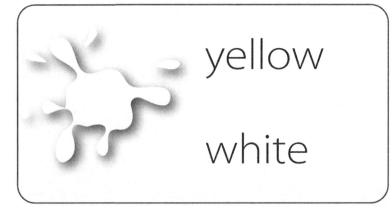

yellow

white

Instructions: *Read the words and draw a line linking up each word with the corresponding pictures.*

 • • white

 • • black

 • • grey

 • • brown

Level 2

At the second level of reading comprehension, children are asked to read some phrases independently, understand their meaning and match them to the pictures. These phrases consist of nouns qualified by adjectives. They are listed in groups.

Fruit:

a red/white/green/yellow lemon

a green/blue/white/red apple

a white/orange/brown/pink orange

a red/white/yellow/grey strawberry

Kitchenware:

a grey/yellow/white/green spoon

a pink/blue/white/orange mug

a yellow/red/brown/white frying pan

a white/grey/green/pink pot

Animals:

a big horse

a little monkey

a little frog

a big cat

a big pig

a little sheep

a big dog

Animals:

a little elephant

a little crab

a little lizard

a big duck

a big butterfly

a little parrot

a big pelican

a big octopus

a little whale

Persons:

a tall man

a short man

a tall woman

a short woman

Hair:

brown hair

blond hair

black hair

a yellow lemon

a red apple

an orange orange

a red strawberry

a red lemon

a green apple

a brown orange

a white strawberry

a white lemon

a blue apple

a white orange

a yellow strawberry

Instructions: *Read the phrase of each box and circle the appropriate picture.*

a green lemon

a white apple

a pink orange

a grey strawberry

Instructions: Read the phrase of each box and circle the appropriate picture.

a yellow spoon

a white mug

a brown frying pan

a green pot

a grey spoon

an orange mug

a yellow frying pan

a white pot

a white spoon

a pink mug

a red frying pan

a grey pot

a green spoon

a blue mug

a white frying pan

a pink pot

Instructions: *Read the phrase of each box and circle the appropriate picture.*

a big horse

a little monkey

a little frog

a big cat

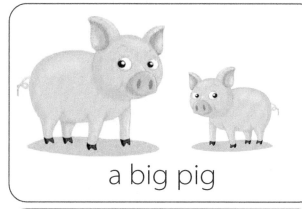

a big pig

a little sheep

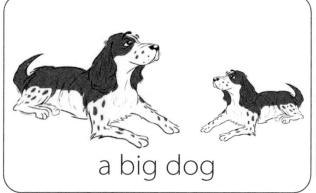

a big dog

a little elephant

a little crab

a little lizard

a big duck

a big butterfly

a little parrot

a big pelican

a big octopus

a little whale

Instructions: *Read the phrase of each box and circle the appropriate picture.*

a tall woman

a short man

a tall man

a short man

a short woman

a tall man

a short man

a tall man

Instructions: *Read the phrase of each box and circle the appropriate picture.*

blond hair

black hair

brown hair

black hair

blond hair

brown hair

black hair

blond hair

Level 3

At the third level of reading comprehension, children are asked to read phrases independently, understand their meaning and match them to the pictures. These phrases are the following:

Professions:

He is a fisherman.

She is a dressmaker.

She is a dancer.

She is a photographer.

She is a hairdresser.

She is a doctor.

She is a teacher.

He is a doctor.

He is a teacher.

She is a pupil.

He is a pupil.

He is a confectioner.

Places:

This is the sea.

This is a forest.

This is a farm.

This is a river.

This is a garden.

This is a meadow.

This is a jungle.

This is a house.

This is a lake.

Animals/Places:

Hippopotamuses live in rivers.

Sheep live in meadows.

Bears live in forests.

Horses live in farms.

Cows live in farms.

Dogs live in houses.

Bees live in gardens.

Lions live in the jungle.

Pigs live in farms.

Fish live in the sea.

Frogs live in lakes.

Birds live in the sky.

He is a fisherman.

She is a dressmaker.

She is a dancer.

She is a photographer.

She is a hairdresser.

She is a doctor.

She is a teacher.

He is a doctor.

He is a teacher.

She is a pupil.

He is a pupil.

He is a confectioner.

This is the sea.

This is a river.

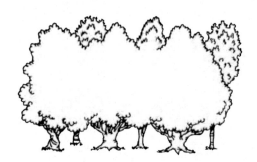

This is a forest.

This is a garden.

This is a meadow.

This is a jungle.

Instructions: *Read the following sentences and circle the appropriate picture.*

This is a house.

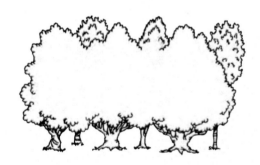

This is a farm.

This is a lake.

Hippopotamuses live in rivers.

Sheep live in meadows.

Bears live in forests.

 Horses live in farms.

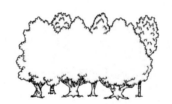

 Cows live in farms.

 Dogs live in houses.

 Bees live in gardens.

 Lions live in the jungle.

 Pigs live in farms.

 Fish live in the sea.

 Frogs live in lakes.

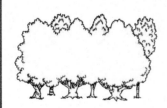  

 Birds live in the sky.

Level 4

At the fourth level of reading comprehension, children are asked to read a four-line text independently (vertical reading. Each line has one sentence). Then they listen to some questions. They are given two answers and are asked to select and circle the correct one. The questions they should answer are the following:

In the first part, there are texts featuring man as the leading character:

1) *Who is the character of the story?*

2) *What is...?*

3) *Where is...?*

4) *What is Mr/Ms X doing? – What has Mr/Ms X done?*

5) *How is Mr/Ms X feeling?*

In the second part, there are texts featuring animals as the leading characters:

1) *Who is the character of the story?*

2) *What is...?*

3) *Where is it?*

4) *What's the colour of...?*

5) *What is it doing?*

Helen is a girl.

Helen is at school.

Helen is playing tennis.

Helen is tired.

Reading comprehension questions

1.	Who is the character of the story?	Is it Maria or Helen?
2.	What is Helen?	Is this child a boy or a girl?
3.	Where is Helen?	Is she at home or at school?
4.	What is Helen doing?	Is she playing basketball or tennis?
5.	How is Helen feeling?	Is she tired or sad?

Sofia is a girl.

Sofia is at the market.

Sofia has bought a present.

Sofia is happy.

Reading comprehension questions

1.	Who is the character of the story?	Is it Sofia or Alice?
2.	What is Sofia?	Is this child a boy or a girl?
3.	Where is Sofia?	Is she at home or at the market?
4.	What has Sofia done?	Has she bought a present or has she gone for a walk?
5.	How is Sofia feeling?	Is she tired or happy?

Myrto is a girl.

Myrto is at school.

Myrto is dancing.

Myrto is happy.

Reading comprehension questions

1. Who is the character of the story?   Is it Clio or Myrto?

2. What is Myrto?   Is this child a boy or a girl?

3. Where is Myrto?   Is she at home or at school?

4. What is Myrto doing?   Is she dancing or singing?

5. How is Myrto feeling?   Is she sad or happy?

Lydia is a girl.

Lydia is at the park.

Lydia is eating ice cream.

Lydia is happy.

Reading comprehension questions

1.	Who is the character of the story?	Is it Sofia or Lydia?
2.	What is Lydia?	Is this child a boy or a girl?
3.	Where is Lydia?	Is she at home or at the park?
4.	What is Lydia doing?	Is she eating ice cream or is she sleeping?
5.	How is Lydia feeling?	Is she sad or happy?

Anna is a girl.

Anna is at the beach.

Anna is swimming.

Anna is happy.

Reading comprehension questions

1.	Who is the character of the story?	Is it Anna or Athena?
2.	What is Anna?	Is this child a boy or a girl?
3.	Where is Anna?	Is she at the beach or on the mountain?
4.	What is Anna doing?	Is she swimming or sleeping?
5.	How is Anna feeling?	Is she sad or happy?

Catherine is a girl.

Catherine is in the kitchen.

Catherine is cooking.

Catherine is happy.

Reading comprehension questions

1.	Who is the character of the story?	Is it Demeter or Catherine?
2.	What is Catherine?	Is this child a boy or a girl?
3.	Where is Catherine?	Is she in the living room or in the kitchen?
4.	What is Catherine doing?	Is she cooking or is she sleeping?
5.	How is Catherine feeling?	Is she sad or happy?

Charlotte is a girl.

Charlotte is at home.

Charlotte has a stomachache.

Charlotte is sad.

Reading comprehension questions

1.	Who is the character of the story?	Is it Emma or Caroline?
2.	What is Charlotte?	Is this child a boy or a girl?
3.	Where is Charlotte?	Is she at home or in the farm?
4.	What is Charlotte doing?	Does she have a stomachache or is she eating?
5.	How is Charlotte feeling?	Is she happy or sad?

Daisy is a girl.

Daisy is at school.

Daisy is writing in the notepad.

Daisy is happy.

Reading comprehension questions

1.	Who is the character of the story?	Is it Angela or Daisy?
2.	What is Daisy?	Is this child a boy or a girl?
3.	Where is Daisy?	Is she at home or at school?
4.	What is Daisy doing?	Is she playing or is she writing?
5.	How is Daisy feeling?	Is she happy or tired?

Maria is a girl.

Maria is at the doctor's office.

Maria is being given an injection.

Maria is scared.

Reading comprehension questions

1.	Who is the character of the story?	Is it Alice or Maria?
2.	What is Maria?	Is this child a boy or a girl?
3.	Where is Maria?	Is she in the garden or at the doctor's office?
4.	What is Maria doing?	Is she being given an injection or is she planting?
5.	How is Maria feeling?	Is she sleepy or scared?

Olivia is a girl.

Olivia is at home.

Olivia is reading a book.

Olivia is sad.

Reading comprehension questions

1.	Who is the character of the story?	Is it Stella or Olivia?
2.	What is Olivia?	Is this child a boy or a girl?
3.	Where is Olivia?	Is she at home or at school?
4.	What is Olivia doing?	Is she reading or is she eating?
5.	How is Olivia feeling?	Is she happy or sad?

Stella is a girl.

Stella is at the hairdresser's.

Stella is having her hair cut.

Stella is happy.

Reading comprehension questions

1.	Who is the character of the story?	Is it Stella or Sofia?
2.	What is Stella?	Is this child a boy or a girl?
3.	Where is Stella?	Is she at the hairdresser's or at the swimming pool?
4.	What is Stella doing?	Is she sleeping or is she having her hair cut?
5.	How is Stella feeling?	Is she happy or sad?

Daisy is a girl.

Daisy is at home.

Daisy is sitting.

Daisy is angry.

Reading comprehension questions

1.	Who is the character of the story?	Is it Maria or is it Daisy?
2.	What is Daisy?	Is this child a boy or a girl?
3.	Where is Daisy?	Is she at home or at school?
4.	What is Daisy doing?	Is she sleeping or is she sitting?
5.	How is Daisy feeling?	Is she angry or happy?

Nick is a boy.

Nick is at the court.

Nick is playing basketball.

Nick is happy.

Reading comprehension questions

1.	Who is the character of the story?	Is it Nick or Peter?
2.	What is Nick?	Is it a boy or a girl?
3.	Where is Nick?	Is he at the court or at home?
4.	What is Nick doing?	Is he playing basketball or is he reading a book?
5.	How is Nick feeling?	Is he sad or happy?

George is a boy.

George is at the court.

George is playing football.

George is angry.

Reading comprehension questions

1.	Who is the character of the story?	Is it John or George?
2.	What is George?	Is this child a boy or a girl?
3.	Where is George?	Is he at the park or at the sports field?
4.	What is George doing?	Is he playing football or is he eating an apple?
5.	How is George feeling?	Is he happy or angry?

Instructions: *Read the text and circle the correct answer.*

John is a boy.

John is at the park.

John is running.

John is tired.

Reading comprehension questions

1. Who is the character of the story?   Is it John or George?
2. What is John?   Is this child a boy or a girl?
3. Where is John?   Is he at the park or at home?
4. What is John doing?   Is he sleeping or is he running?
5. How is John feeling?   Is he happy or sad?

Bill is a boy.

Bill is at school.

Bill has got a medal.

Bill is happy.

Reading comprehension questions

1.	Who is the character of the story?	Is it Bill or William?
2.	What is Bill?	Is this child a boy or a girl?
3.	Where is Bill?	Is he at school or at home?
4.	What has Bill done?	Has he got a bag or a medal?
5.	How is Bill feeling?	Is he sad or happy?

William is a boy.

William is in the forest.

William is photographing birds.

William is happy.

Reading comprehension questions

1. Who is the character of the story?   Is it John or William?
2. What is William?   Is this child a boy or a girl?
3. Where is William?   Is he at school or in the forest?
4. What is William doing?   Is he sleeping or is he photographing birds?
5. How is William feeling?   Is he happy or sad?

Liam is a boy.

Liam is in the bus.

Liam is listening to music.

Liam is happy.

Reading comprehension questions

1.	Who is the character of the story?	Is it Liam or Nick?
2.	What is Liam?	Is this child a boy or a girl?
3.	Where is Liam?	Is he in the bus or at home?
4.	What is Liam doing?	Is he reading a book or is he listening to music?
5.	How is Liam feeling?	Is he sad or happy?

Ethan is a boy.

Ethan is at the river.

Ethan is holding a fish.

Ethan is happy.

Reading comprehension questions

1.	Who is the character of the story?	Is it John or Ethan?
2.	What is Ethan?	Is this child a boy or a girl?
3.	Where is Ethan?	Is he at the lake or at the river?
4.	What is Ethan doing?	Is he holding a fish or is he swimming?
5.	How is Ethan feeling?	Is he sad or happy?

Jim is a boy.

Jim is at home.

Jim got a present.

Jim is happy.

Reading comprehension questions

1.	Who is the character of the story?	Is it Jim or George?
2.	What is Jim?	Is this child a boy or a girl?
3.	Where is Jim?	Is he at home or at school?
4.	What is Jim doing?	Is he dancing or did he get a present?
5.	How is Jim feeling?	Is he happy or sad?

Peter is a boy.

Peter is in the park.

Peter is playing with the little dogs.

Peter is happy.

Reading comprehension questions

1.	Who is the character of the story?	Is it Peter or Nick?
2.	What is Peter?	Is it a girl or is it a boy?
3.	Where is Peter?	Is he at the park or at home?
4.	What is Peter doing?	Is he playing with the little dogs or with the kittens?
5.	How is Peter feeling?	Is he sad or happy?

Oliver is a boy.

Oliver is at the doctor's office.

Oliver is being given an injection.

Oliver is afraid.

Reading comprehension questions

1. Who is the character of the story?   Is it John or Oliver?

2. What is Oliver?   Is this child a boy or a girl?

3. Where is Oliver?   Is he at school or at the doctor's office?

4. What is Oliver doing?   Is he playing football or is he being given an injection?

5. How is Oliver feeling?   Is he afraid or sleepy?

Daniel is a boy.

Daniel is at home.

Daniel is having a bad dream.

Daniel is scared.

Reading comprehension questions

1.	Who is the character of the story?	Is it Nick or Daniel?
2.	What is Daniel?	Is this child a boy or a girl?
3.	Where is Daniel?	Is he at home or at school?
4.	What is Daniel doing?	Is he eating a banana or is he having a bad dream?
5.	How is Daniel feeling?	Is he scared or happy?

Elijah is a boy.

Elijah is on the mountain.

Elijah is wearing a jacket.

Elijah is tired.

Reading comprehension questions

1.	Who is the character of the story?	Is it Charles or Elijah?
2.	What is Elijah?	Is this child a boy or a girl?
3.	Where is Elijah?	Is he at the supermarket or on the mountain?
4.	What is Elijah doing?	Is he wearing a jacket or a cap?
5.	How is Elijah feeling?	Is he sad or tired?

A swallow is a bird.

The swallow is in the sky.

The swallow is black and white.

The swallow is flying.

Reading comprehension questions

1.	Who is the character of the story?	Is it the swallow or the rooster?
2.	What is a swallow?	Is it a bird or a fish?
3.	Where is the swallow?	Is it by the sea or in the sky?
4.	What's the colour of the swallow?	Is it white and red or black and white?
5.	What is the swallow doing?	Is it flying or is it swimming?

A canary is a bird.

The canary is on the branch.

The canary is yellow.

The canary is flying.

Reading comprehension questions

1. Who is the character of the story?   Is it the duck or the canary?

2. What is a canary?   Is it a bird or a fish?

3. Where is the canary?   Is it on the rock or on the branch?

4. What's the colour of the canary?   Is it green or yellow?

5. What is the canary doing?   Is it swimming or is it flying?

A crocodile is an animal.

The crocodile is in the boat.

The crocodile is green.

The crocodile is swimming.

Reading comprehension questions

1.	Who is the character of the story?	Is it the crocodile or the rooster?
2.	What is a crocodile?	Is it an animal or a man?
3.	Where is the crocodile?	Is it in the car or in the boat?
4.	What's the colour of the crocodile?	Is it green or red?
5.	What is the crocodile doing?	Is it flying or is it swimming?

A frog is an animal.

The frog is in the lake.

The frog is green.

The frog is swimming.

Reading comprehension questions

1.	Who is the character of the story?	Is it the duck or the frog?
2.	What is a frog?	Is it an animal or a fruit?
3.	Where is the frog?	Is it in the sea or in the lake?
4.	What's the colour of the frog?	Is it red or green?
5.	What is the frog doing?	Is it flying or is it swimming?

A dolphin is an animal.

The dolphin is in the sea.

The dolphin is grey.

The dolphin is swimming.

Reading comprehension questions

1.	Who is the character of the story?	Is it the octopus or the dolphin?
2.	What is a dolphin?	Is it a child or an animal?
3.	Where is the dolphin?	Is it in the sea or in the sky?
4.	What's the colour of the dolphin?	Is it yellow or grey?
5.	What is the dolphin doing?	Is it flying or is it swimming?

An octopus is an animal.

The octopus is in the sea.

The octopus is pink.

The octopus is swimming.

Reading comprehension questions

1.	Who is the character of the story?	Is it the cat or the octopus?
2.	What is an octopus?	Is it an animal or a vegetable?
3.	Where is the octopus?	Is it in the sky or in the sea?
4.	What's the colour of the octopus?	Is it blue or pink?
5.	What is the octopus doing?	Is it swimming or is it flying?

An elephant is an animal.

The elephant is in the forest.

The elephant is grey.

The elephant is walking.

Reading comprehension questions

1. Who is the character of the story?   Is it the elephant or the crocodile?

2. What is an elephant?   Is it an animal or a fruit?

3. Where is the elephant?   Is it in the sea or in the forest?

4. What's the colour of the elephant?   Is it red or grey?

5. What is the elephant doing?   Is it walking or is it swimming?

A zebra is an animal.

The zebra is in the forest.

The zebra is black and white.

The zebra is running.

Reading comprehension questions

1.	Who is the character of the story?	Is it the zebra or the lion?
2.	What is a zebra?	Is it a piece of clothes or is it an animal?
3.	Where is the zebra?	Is it in the forest or in the sea?
4.	What's the colour of the zebra?	Is it white and blue or black and white?
5.	What is the zebra doing?	Is it flying or is it running?

Instructions: *Read the text and circle the correct answer.*

A monkey is an animal.

The monkey is in the forest.

The monkey is brown.

The monkey is climbing.

Reading comprehension questions

1.	Who is the character of the story?	Is it the cat or the monkey?
2.	What is a monkey?	Is it an animal or an object?
3.	Where is the monkey?	Is it in the forest or in the sky?
4.	What's the colour of the monkey?	Is it yellow or brown?
5.	What is the monkey doing?	Is it climbing or is it swimming?

A goat is an animal.

The goat is in the meadow.

The goat is brown.

The goat is walking.

Reading comprehension questions

1.	Who is the character of the story?	Is it the sheep or the goat?
2.	What is a goat?	Is it an animal or a fruit?
3.	Where is the goat?	Is it in the sea or in the forest?
4.	What's the colour of the goat?	Is it brown or red?
5.	What is the goat doing?	Is it flying or is it walking?

Level 5

At the fifth level of reading comprehension, children are asked to read a four-line text independently (vertical reading. Each line has one sentence). Then they listen to five questions, answer them and write down their answers. The questions they should answer are the following:

In the first part, there are texts featuring man as the leading character:
1) Who is the character of the story?
2) What is...?
3) Where is...?
4) What is Mr/Ms X doing?
5) How is Mr/Ms X feeling?

In the second part, there are texts featuring animals as the leading characters:
1) Who is the character of the story?
2) What is...?
3) Where is it?
4) What's the colour of...?
5) What is it doing?

Mary is a girl.

Mary is at home.

Mary is opening the presents.

Mary is happy.

Reading comprehension questions

1. Who is the character of the story? _____

2. What is Mary? _____

3. Where is Mary? _____

4. What is Mary doing? _____

5. How is Mary feeling? _____

Instructions: *Read the text and answer the questions.*

Mama is a girl.

Mama is at home.

Mama is reading a fairy tale.

Mama is happy.

Reading comprehension questions

1. Who is the character of the story? _____

2. What is mama?   _____

3. Where is mama?   _____

4. What is mama doing?   _____

5. How is mama feeling?   _____

Helen is a girl.

Helen is in the living room.

Helen is watching TV.

Helen is sad.

Reading comprehension questions

1. Who is the character of the story? _____

2. What is Helen? _____

3. Where is Helen? _____

4. What is Helen doing? _____

5. How is Helen feeling? _____

Helle is a girl.

Helle is in the garden.

Helle is watering the flowers.

Helle is happy.

Reading comprehension questions

1. Who is the character of the story? _____

2. What is Helle? _____

3. Where is Helle? _____

4. What is Helle doing? _____

5. How is Helle feeling? _____

Grace is a girl.

Grace is in the kitchen.

Grace is eating food.

Grace is sad.

Reading comprehension questions

1. Who is the character of the story? _____
2. What is Grace? _____
3. Where is Grace? _____
4. What is Grace doing? _____
5. How is Grace feeling? _____

Layla is a girl.

Layla is in the park.

Layla is playing with the ball.

Layla is happy.

Reading comprehension questions

1. Who is the character of the story? _____

2. What is Layla? _____

3. Where is Layla? _____

4. What is Layla doing? _____

5. How is Layla feeling? _____

Nicole is a girl.

Nicole is on the mountain.

Nicole is skiing.

Nicole is happy.

Reading comprehension questions

1. Who is the character of the story? _____

2. What is Nicole? _____

3. Where is Nicole? _____

4. What is Nicole doing? _____

5. How is Nicole feeling? _____

Charles is a boy.

Charles is at home.

Charles got a bird.

Charles is happy.

Reading comprehension questions

1. Who is the character of the story? _____

2. What is Charles? _____

3. Where is Charles? _____

4. What is Charles doing? _____

5. How is Charles feeling? _____

Leo is a boy.

Leo is in the room.

Leo is playing with the toys.

Leo is happy.

Reading comprehension questions

1. Who is the character of the story? _____
2. What is Leo? _____
3. Where is Leo? _____
4. What is Leo doing? _____
5. How is Leo feeling? _____

Stephen is a boy.

Stephen is at work.

Stephen is drinking coffee.

Stephen is tired.

Reading comprehension questions

1. Who is the character of the story? _____

2. What is Stephen? _____

3. Where is Stephen? _____

4. What is Stephen doing? _____

5. How is Stephen feeling? _____

Jace is a boy.

Jace is at home.

Jace is holding a pillow.

Jace is sad.

Reading comprehension questions

1. Who is the character of the story? _____
2. What is Jace? _____
3. Where is Jace? _____
4. What is Jace doing? _____
5. How is Jace feeling? _____

Xavier is a boy.

Xavier is at work.

Xavier is tearing the piece of paper.

Xavier is angry.

Reading comprehension questions

1. Who is the character of the story? _____

2. What is Xavier? _____

3. Where is Xavier? _____

4. What is Xavier doing? _____

5. How is Xavier feeling? _____

Nolan is a boy.

Nolan is in the sea.

Nolan is swimming.

Nolan is tired.

Reading comprehension questions

1. Who is the character of the story? _____

2. What is Nolan? _____

3. Where is Nolan? _____

4. What is Nolan doing? _____

5. How is Nolan feeling? _____

David is a boy.

David is at school.

David broke the pencil.

David is sad.

Reading comprehension questions

1. Who is the character of the story? _____

2. What is David? _____

3. Where is David? _____

4. What is David doing? _____

5. How is David feeling? _____

A whale is an animal.

The whale is in the sea.

The whale is blue.

The whale is swimming.

Reading comprehension questions

1. Who is the character of the story? _____

2. What is a whale? _____

3. Where is the whale? _____

4. What's the colour of the whale? _____

5. What is the whale doing? _____

A crab is an animal.

The crab is in the sea.

The crab is orange.

The crab is walking.

Reading comprehension questions

1. Who is the character of the story? _____

2. What is a crab? _____

3. Where is the crab? _____

4. What's the colour of the crab? _____

5. What is the crab doing? _____

A duck is an animal.

The duck is in the river.

The duck is white.

The duck is swimming.

Reading comprehension questions

1. Who is the character of the story? _____

2. What is a duck? _____

3. Where is the duck? _____

4. What's the colour of the duck? _____

5. What is the duck doing? _____

A pelican is an animal.

The pelican is in the lake.

The pelican is white.

The pelican is flying.

Reading comprehension questions

1. Who is the character of the story? _____

2. What is the pelican? _____

3. Where is the pelican? _____

4. What's the colour of the pelican? _____

5. What is the pelican doing? _____

A lizard is an animal.

The lizard is in the forest.

The lizard is orange.

The lizard is walking.

Reading comprehension questions

1. Who is the character of the story? _____

2. What is a lizard? _____

3. Where is the lizard? _____

4. What's the colour of the lizard? _____

5. What is the lizard doing? _____

A parrot is an animal.

The parrot is in the sky.

The parrot has many colours.

The parrot is flying.

Reading comprehension questions

1. Who is the character of the story? _____

2. What is a parrot? _____

3. Where is the parrot? _____

4. What's the colour of the parrot? _____

5. What is the parrot doing? _____

A butterfly is an animal.

The butterfly is in the sky.

The butterfly has many colours.

The butterfly is flying.

Reading comprehension questions

1.   Who is the character of the story? _____

2.   What is a butterfly?   _____

3.   Where is the butterfly?   _____

4.   What's the colour of the butterfly?_____

5.   What is the butterfly doing?   _____

A cat is an animal.

The cat is at home.

The cat is brown.

The cat is walking.

Reading comprehension questions

1. Who is the character of the story? _____

2. What is the cat? _____

3. Where is the cat? _____

4. What's the colour of the cat? _____

5. What is the cat doing? _____

Level 6

At the sixth level of reading comprehension, children are asked to read a text of six sentences independently. They listen to or read seven questions themselves, answer them and write down their answers. The questions they should answer are the following:

In the first part, there are texts featuring man as the leading character:

1) *Who is the character of the story?*

2) *What is...?*

3) *How is....?*

4) *What is Mr X/Ms Y wearing?*

5) *What is Mr X/Ms Y holding?*

6) *What does Mr X/Ms Y do for a living?*

7) *How is Mr X/Ms Y feeling?*

In the second part, there are texts featuring animals as the leading characters:

1) *Who is the character of the story?*

2) *What's the colour of...?*

3) *How is...?*

4) *What has...?*

5) *Where does this animal live?*

6) *What is this animal doing?*

7) *How is this animal feeling?*

This is Nick. This is a man. He is tall and blond. He is wearing a hat and holding a pair of binoculars. Nick is a fisherman. He is happy.

Reading comprehension questions

1. Who is the character of the story? _____

2. What is Nick? _____

3. How is Nick? _____

4. What is Nick wearing? _____

5. What is Nick holding? _____

6. What does Nick do for a living? _____

7. How is Nick feeling? _____

This is Stella. This is a woman. She is thin and has short hair. She is wearing a dress and is holding a little dog. Stella is a teacher. She is happy.

Reading comprehension questions

1. Who is the character of the story? _____
2. What is Stella? _____
3. How is Stella? _____
4. What is Stella wearing? _____
5. What is Stella holding? _____
6. What does Stella do for a living? _____
7. How is Stella feeling? _____

This is Rosa. She is a woman. She is tall and has black hair. She is wearing a blouse and is holding a bag. Rosa is a dressmaker. She is happy.

Reading comprehension questions

1. Who is the character of the story? _____
2. What is Rosa? _____
3. How is Rosa? _____
4. What is Rosa wearing? _____
5. What is Rosa holding? _____
6. What does Rosa do for a living? _____
7. How is Rosa feeling? _____

This is Nina. She is a woman. She is tall and has brown hair. She is wearing a swimsuit and is holding her flippers. Nina is a dancer. She is happy.

Reading comprehension questions

1. Who is the character of the story? _____
2. What is Nina? _____
3. How is Nina? _____
4. What is Nina wearing? _____
5. What is Nina holding? _____
6. What does Nina do for a living? _____
7. How is Nina feeling? _____

This is Erin. She is a woman. She is thin and blonde. She is wearing a blouse and is holding flowers. Erin is a doctor. She is happy.

Reading comprehension questions

1. Who is the character of the story? _____

2. What is Erin? _____

3. How is Erin? _____

4. What is Erin wearing? _____

5. What is Erin holding? _____

6. What does Erin do for a living? _____

7. How is Erin feeling? _____

This is Lisa. She is a woman. She is thin and blonde. She is wearing a jacket and is holding a cup. Lisa is a secretary. She is tired.

Reading comprehension questions

1. Who is the character of the story? _____
2. What is Lisa? _____
3. How is Lisa? _____
4. What is Lisa wearing? _____
5. What is Lisa holding? _____
6. What does Lisa do for a living? _____
7. How is Lisa feeling? _____

This is Anna. She is a woman. She is tall and blonde. She is wearing a black blouse and is holding a photo. Anna is a photographer. She is angry.

Reading comprehension questions

1. Who is the character of the story? _____
2. What is Anna? _____
3. How is Anna? _____
4. What is Anna wearing? _____
5. What is Anna holding? _____
6. What does Anna do for a living? _____
7. How is Anna feeling? _____

This is Charles. He is a man. He is tall and has brown hair. He is wearing a sweater is holding his mobile phone. Charles is a teacher. He is sad.

Reading comprehension questions

1. Who is the character of the story? _____
2. What is Charles? _____
3. How is Charles? _____
4. What is Charles wearing? _____
5. What is Charles holding? _____
6. What does Charles do for a living? _____
7. How is Charles feeling? _____

This is Ashley. She is a girl. She is thin and blonde. She is wearing a yellow blouse and is holding a bag. Ashley is a pupil. She is sad.

Reading comprehension questions

1. Who is the character of the story? _____
2. What is Ashley? _____
3. How is Ashley? _____
4. What is Ashley wearing? _____
5. What is Ashley holding? _____
6. What does Ashley do for a living? _____
7. How is Ashley feeling? _____

This is Jim. He is a man. He is tall and blond. He is wearing a T-shirt and is holding a cup of tea. Jim is a confectioner. He is happy.

Reading comprehension questions

1. Who is the character of the story? _____

2. What is Jim? _____

3. How is Jim? _____

4. What is Jim wearing? _____

5. What is Jim holding? _____

6. What does Jim do for a living? _____

7. How is Jim feeling? _____

This is Irena. She is a woman. She is tall and blonde. She is wearing a white blouse and is holding a bottle of nail polish. Irena is a hairdresser. She is happy.

Reading comprehension questions

1. Who is the character of the story? _____
2. What is Irena? _____
3. How is Irena feeling? _____
4. What is Irena wearing? _____
5. What is Irena holding? _____
6. What does Irena do for a living? _____
7. How is Irena feeling? _____

This is Catherine. She is a woman. She is tall and has long hair. She is wearing a pink blouse and is holding a book. Catherine is a teacher. She is scared.

Reading comprehension questions

1. Who is the character of the story? _____
2. What is Catherine? _____
3. How is Catherine? _____
4. What is Catherine wearing? _____
5. What is Catherine holding? _____
6. What does Catherine do for a living? _____
7. How is Catherine feeling? _____

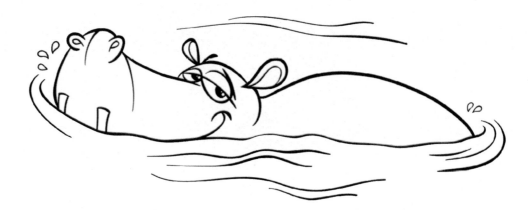

This is a hippopotamus. The hippopotamus is grey. It is big and has small ears. It lives in the river. It is swimming. It is happy.

Reading comprehension questions

1. Who is the character of the story? _____
2. What's the colour of the hippopotamus? _____
3. How is the hippopotamus? _____
4. What does the hippopotamus have? _____
5. Where does the hippopotamus live? _____
6. What is the hippopotamus doing? _____
7. How is the hippopotamus feeling? _____

This is a sheep. The sheep is white. It is small and has thin legs. It lives in the meadow. The sheep is drinking water. It is happy.

Reading comprehension questions

1. Who is the character of the story? _____
2. What's the colour of the sheep? _____
3. How is the sheep? _____
4. What does the sheep have? _____
5. Where is the sheep living? _____
6. What is the sheep doing? _____
7. How is the sheep feeling? _____

This is a bear. The bear is brown. The bear is big and has big legs. It lives in the forest. The bear is eating honey. It is happy.

Reading comprehension questions

1. Who is the character of the story?

2. What's the colour of the bear?

3. How is the bear?

4. What does the bear have?

5. Where does the bear live?

6. What is the bear doing?

7. How is the bear feeling?

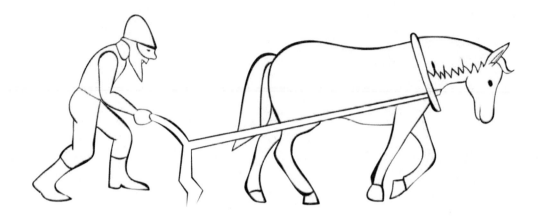

This is a horse. The horse is brown. It is big and has a long tail. It lives in the farm. The horse is plowing the field. It is tired.

Reading comprehension questions

1. Who is the character of the story?
2. What's the colour of the horse?
3. How is the horse?
4. What does the horse have?
5. Where does the horse live?
6. What is the horse doing?
7. How is the horse feeling?

This is a cow. The cow is black and white.

It is big and has horns. It lives in the farm.

The cow is eating. It is happy.

Reading comprehension questions

1. Who is the character of the story?
2. What is the colour of the cow?
3. How is the cow?
4. What does the cow have?
5. Where does the cow live?
6. What is the cow doing?
7. How is the cow feeling?

This is a dog. The dog is brown. It is small and has big ears. It lives in the garden. The dog is sitting. It is sad.

Reading comprehension questions

1. Who is the character of the story?
2. What's the colour of the dog?
3. How is the dog?
4. What does the dog have?
5. Where does the dog live?
6. What is the dog doing?
7. How is the dog feeling?

This is a bee. The bee is yellow and black. It is small and has wings. It lives in the garden. The bee is flying. It is angry.

Reading comprehension questions

1. Who is the character of the story?
2. What's the colour of the bee?
3. How is the bee?
4. What does the bee have?
5. Where does the bee live?
6. What is the bee doing?
7. How is the bee feeling?

This is a pig. The pig is pink. The pig is fat and has a small tail. It lives in the farm. The pig is hiding. It is scared.

Reading comprehension questions

1. Who is the character of the story?
2. What's the colour of the frog?
3. How is the frog?
4. What does the frog have?
5. Where does the pig live?
6. What is the pig doing?
7. How is the pig feeling?

This is a dog. The dog is red. It is small and has big eyes. It lives in the house. The dog is running. It is scared.

Reading comprehension questions

1. Who is the character of the story?
2. What's the colour of the dog?
3. How is the dog?
4. What does the dog have?
5. Where does the dog live?
6. What is the dog doing?
7. How is the dog feeling?

This is a lion. The lion is orange. It is big and has a thin tail. It lives in the jungle. The lion is sleeping. It is tired.

Reading comprehension questions

1. Who is the character of the story?
2. What is the colour of the lion?
3. How is the lion?
4. What does the lion have?
5. Where does the lion live?
6. What is the lion doing?
7. How is the lion feeling?

This is a frog. The frog is green. It is small and has a big tongue. It lives in the lake, next to a flower. The frog is running. It is scared.

Reading comprehension questions

1. Who is the character of the story? _____
2. What's the colour of the frog? _____
3. How is the frog? _____
4. What does the frog have? _____
5. Where does the frog live? _____
6. What is the frog doing? _____
7. How is the frog feeling? _____

This is a fish. The fish is red. It is big and has a long tail. It lives in the sea, next to a plant. The fish is swimming. It is happy.

Reading comprehension questions

1. Who is the character of the story?
2. What's the colour of the fish?
3. How is the fish?
4. What does the fish have?
5. Where does the fish live?
6. What is the fish doing?
7. How is the fish feeling?

Printed in Great Britain
by Amazon

25782579R00084